Canadian Critical Issues Series

The Canadian Critical Issues Series has grown out of the Canadian Public Issues Project, which was initiated at the Ontario Institute for Studies in Education early in the summer of 1969 by John Eisenberg, Malcolm Levin, and Lionel Orlikow. The purpose of the project was to stimulate discussion and reflection about controversial issues in contemporary Canadian society by developing a program focusing on these issues through case studies about various social problems in Canada. Since 1969 the staff of the Canadian Public Issues Project has researched and collected materials, and written cases about contemporary incidents under a wide range of problem areas, including Canadian–U.S. relations; law enforcement methods; birth control, abortion, and euthanasia; "forbidden" topics in school curricula; rights of youth; labour and the right to strike; separatism in Quebec and elsewhere; and minority group rights. The cases are, for the most part, based on published reports in various newspapers, journals, books, legal documents, and government reports. Many of the cases have been organized into topical "units" and have been taught experimentally in high-school classrooms in Metropolitan Toronto, Belleville, Ottawa, and elsewhere in Canada. The books in the Canadian Critical Issues Series are adapted from these units.

The books are intended to be both provocative and informative. Case studies are followed· by questions and analogy situations designed to stimulate reflection and discussion about the case and about the broader issues it raises. Additional factual information and, in some instances, interpretive essays are included to bring other perspectives to bear on the cases and the problems they represent. Each book concludes with a selected bibliography of reference and resource materials in print and on film and tape. It is hoped that these books will contribute to fruitful dialogue among students, teachers, and the reading public about some of the conditions and problems of growing up, getting an education, and working and living in Canada today.

This series would not have been possible without the funds allocated within O.I.S.E. to the Canadian Public Issues Project since 1969. We especially wish to acknowledge the support and assistance given by John Main of the Editorial Division, Ralph Garry of the Department of Curriculum, and Clive Beck of the Department of History and Philosophy of Education. We also wish to thank the many graduate students at O.I.S.E. and high-school teachers who assisted in the research and in teaching and evaluating case materials for the project. Finally, in addition to the project research staff – Paula Bourne, Marion Harris, and Christine Sylvester – we are especially indebted to Peggy Bristow for her assistance in typing and retyping the final manuscripts for the books in this series.

John A. Eisenberg
Malcolm A. Levin
Editors, Canadian Critical Issues Series

Don't Teach That!

John Eisenberg & Gailand MacQueen
with the assistance of
**Marion Harris, Paula Bourne, &
Christine Sylvester**

PaperJacks

*A division of General Publishing Co. Limited
Don Mills, Ontario*

First published by PaperJacks
A division of General Publishing Co. Limited,
30 Lesmill Road, Don Mills, Ontario

ISBN 0-7737-7012-7

ACKNOWLEDGMENTS: excerpts from Letters to the Editor, *Calgary Herald* (pages 7, 23-9), reprinted with permission of the Calgary Herald. Thomas Allen (pages 78-80) reprinted by permission of the Toronto Star; Pierre Berton (pages 87-8) reprinted by permission of the author.

Printed and bound in Canada
by John Deyell Limited

CONTENTS

Introduction/7

I. SEX EDUCATION

"Gross Misconduct" in Moosomin/10

The Calgary Sex Education Controversy/21

II. POLITICS IN THE SCHOOLS

The Political Beliefs of Teachers/38

Peace Club/48

Discussion of Vietnam/54

III. RELIGION AND EDUCATION

The Case of Paul Peterson/60

The Case of Gertrude Conrad/73

Separate Schools – Manitoba's

Ticking Time-Bomb/78

The Role of Government/89

Bibliography/102

INTRODUCTION

In a letter to the *Calgary Herald,* on April 29, 1969, Reita Vance said: "Certainly a parent has always had the right and privilege of teaching his culture, his beliefs and his religion to his offspring."

However, governments, in instituting religious and sex education programs, have also laid claim to this right as part of their responsibility for training future citizens. An example of this is the program of religious and sex education in Ontario. Moreover, governments have assumed the task of teaching political responsibilities in civics courses and, in some cases, have determined that certain beliefs make individuals unfit to teach the young.

Because of conflicting claims to this right, disputes have arisen, are arising, and will continue to arise in the future.

The issue is: Who has the right to teach sexual, political, and religious beliefs to children?

I

SEX EDUCATION

"GROSS MISCONDUCT" IN MOOSOMIN

Moosomin, Saskatchewan, is a small prairie town with a population of about 3,000 people. It is situated along the Trans-Canada Highway, 140 miles east of Regina, near the Manitoba border. By so-called big-city standards, the attitudes of many of the inhabitants of Moosomin are conservative. Modern ideas about drugs, sexual freedom, and absence of authority for the young are especially unacceptable to these individuals.

Until October 1971, twenty-four-year-old Mrs. Margaret Gordon was a home economics teacher at McNaughton High School in Moosomin. To those people holding traditional rural values and opposing some of the modern trends, Mrs. Gordon would likely appear unconventional. During the summer her husband often picked up young hitch-hikers along the Trans-Canada Highway, whom the Gordons would put up overnight at their farm, and they often discussed problems affecting these young people late into the night. Mrs. Gordon also worked as an organizer for the N.D.P. in the 1971 provincial election and supported the radical Waffle wing of that party. And she favoured free discussion of topics some people would consider to be in bad taste. It was therefore understandable that a storm would result when the different basic attitudes crossed in Moosomin.

Mrs. Gordon was in her second year of teaching on a probationary certificate at the school when the conflict arose. Until that time she had gotten along well in the school and her work was considered to be "very satisfactory". She tried out new programs and encouraged student interest in modern social issues. In her homeroom periods she would go beyond the regular school program and hold informal discussions on controversial matters with her Grade 9 class. Students could talk openly and frankly on drugs, presenting their own views on the subject and not merely stating what they believed the teachers would approve. According to Mrs. Gordon, these discussions were "great".

One day late in September, she brought several copies of the Vancouver underground newspaper *Georgia Straight* to her class. She believed that some of the articles expressed ideas that could be used for class discussions. In one issue of the paper there was a detailed description of a young girl's first sexual experience, an article on how to rebel against a high school, and an article on how teachers can undermine the school system.

A crisis quickly developed when the mother of one student saw the copy of the *Georgia Straight* that her son brought home. She was outraged to see the contents of the newspaper used in school, especially the intimate account of the young girl's sexual experiences, and notified the principal of her thoughts and feelings. A meeting between Mrs. Gordon, the principal of McNaughton High School, the school superintendent for the district, and the chairman of the district board of education was then called. At this meeting Mrs. Gordon was asked to stop bringing the *Georgia Straight* to school, to stop discussing controversial issues not prescribed in the school curriculum, and to apologize to a meeting of parents for her actions.

Mr. Donald Keith, executive assistant of the Saskatchewan Teachers' Federation, met with the parents first in order to arrange such a meeting. He attempted to explain what Mrs. Gordon was trying to do in her homeroom classes and why she had used the underground newspaper. However, the parents were not persuaded by Mr. Keith and were not willing to meet with Mrs. Gordon. They instead recommended to the board that she be fired. Shortly thereafter, Mrs. Gordon was dismissed by the local school board for "gross misconduct" under the provisions of the School Act.

While the uproar was raging in and about Moosomin, rumours were spreading rapidly and may have added fuel to the controversy. According to one rumour, Mrs. Gordon supported the taking of drugs. More seriously, other rumours claimed that she was to be dismissed for selling drugs to students, and even that she had injected LSD into cubes of sugar at the school. However, Mrs. Gordon vigorously denied all of these reports, asserting that they were totally unfounded.

Soon after Mrs. Gordon received the notice of dismissal, she filed an appeal with the Department of Education. This Department decided that under the circumstances it would be best to set up a committee of inquiry to investigate the dismissal and the factors leading up to it. Because the case engendered such strong feelings and became so explosive, the three members of the committee decided to hold a closed inquiry.

In all, more than twenty witnesses testified at the closed hearings. Some defended the right of a teacher to discuss freely delicate subjects in a classroom. On the other hand, the more conservative citizens were bewildered and felt threatened by the new influences their children were being subjected to. They feared that their children would be corrupted by the new ideas about drugs and sex. Some even threatened to keep their children out of school if Mrs. Gordon were permitted to teach again.

After reviewing the testimony carefully, the committee of inquiry sent its recommendations to Mr. Gordon MacMurchy, Minister of Education of Saskatchewan. Then on January 4, 1972, he stated his decision publicly, ordering the Moosomin School Unit Board to withdraw charges of gross misconduct against Mrs. Gordon and to set aside her dismissal on the basis of those charges.

Although he overturned the school board's verdict against Mrs. Gordon, Mr. MacMurchy was critical of the use in a Grade 9 class of the article in the *Georgia Straight* describing the sexual experiences of a young girl. He said: "In my view, if the article in question was made available to students it was a clear transgression of community standards. While it is the job of teachers to help students examine and challenge the world around them, there are bounds of good taste and there are limits to what material might be considered useful in the school setting."

However, it must be noted that, despite his order to withdraw charges of gross misconduct against Mrs.

Gordon, Mr. MacMurchy did not order her rein- statement. The Minister avoided making any clear and definite statement on this matter by saying that any further action would be left to the school board and Mrs. Gordon to work out.

But prospects for Mrs. Gordon's return to her Moosomin classes were very dim indeed. At both the local and unit levels, members of the school board opposed her return. Mrs. James Ingram, chairman of the Moosomin Board of Education, made it clear that Mrs. Gordon would not return as a teacher because the board was against such a step. Mr. John Jackson of the School Unit Board lent some support to this view by saying that the com- munity was not anxious to have Mrs. Gordon back as a teacher. And despite a court ruling that Mr. MacMurchy had the right to instruct the board to dismiss charges of gross misconduct, the board, supported by the Saskatchewan School Trustees' Association, considered appealing the court decision. They believed "the outcome will determine whether parents and the community have a right to determine who shall teach their children and what their children shall be taught".

On hearing the remarks of the Minister of Educa- tion, Mrs. Gordon was disappointed. In spite of her "victory" in having the charges withdrawn, she saw little chance of her continuing on as a teacher. For she realized that she could be dismissed under a dif- ferent section of the School Act, or that she could be paid by the Moosomin board till the end of the school year and then not be re-hired the next year. As she summarized, "It looks like the end of my teaching career."

The Issues

- Should Margaret Gordon be reinstated as a teacher in Moosomin?

Georgia Straight *in the classroom*

- Should Mrs. Gordon have brought issues of the *Georgia Straight,* especially the issue objected to by parents, into her Grade 9 class?

- Should she have restricted to class time the reading and discussion of the articles in question, and not allowed students to take copies of the *Georgia Straight* home?

- Would her actions have been more acceptable if her homeroom class had been Grade 12 students? adults in a night-school class?

- Would it have been more proper if Mrs. Gordon had discussed "explosive" topics with groups of males and females separately? If you believe so, do you also believe that the discussion of Christian beliefs should be held in separate groups of Christians, Jews, agnostics, atheists? Or, in the discussion of the Reformation in history courses, should classes be divided into Protestants, Roman Catholics, and other groups? Why?

Sensitive topics in the curriculum

- Should Mrs. Gordon have used her home-period

classes for discussion of such controversial subjects as drugs and sex?

- Do you believe that the discussion of such topics is better treated in health, biology, or physical education classes than in homeroom classes? On what grounds would you defend your position?

- Which of the following sensitive topics do you believe should be discussed as part of the school curriculum: religion; ethics; politics; sex; death; witchcraft; superstition? Are there any topics which you believe should not be treated in the classroom? If so, why?

- Should the Department of Education set down clearly which topics are to be studied and discussed and which are not?

Community standards and educational values

- Is a teacher ever justified in encouraging free discussion of topics that are considered too controversial for classroom discussion by a sizeable part of the community?

- If the curriculum set by the Department of Education violates local community standards of good taste or "truth", should the teacher be permitted to avoid treating such topics? Would a member of the Jehovah's Witness sect be justified in keeping his fourteen-year-old son home while the theory of evolution, part of the official curriculum, was being taught? Would an atheist be justified in keeping his child home if he knew that a Christian Evangelist was to address a compulsory school assembly?

- If it could be shown that students' understanding of important issues would be increased by discussing such articles as those presented in the *Georgia Straight,* which articles would you consider proper and which improper for classroom use: the description of a young girl's sexual experiences; ways in which students can rebel against the high school; ways in which teachers can disrupt the school system?

- If it could be shown that students' understanding was improved by free classroom discussions about sex, would such discussions be justified even when they affected student attitudes in a way parents did not approve of?

- If student sexual behaviour were affected in a way that parents disapproved of, should free discussions of sex be permitted?

"Good taste"

- If Mrs. Gordon sincerely believed that the free and open discussion of drugs and sex would benefit her students in terms of both valuable knowledge and healthier attitudes, would she be guilty of violating standards of good taste in Moosomin?

ANALOGY. In the Slippery Plains High School in Manitoba, not far across the border from Moosomin, *Catcher in the Rye,* by J. D. Salinger, was put on the required reading list in English for Grade 11 students. Some parents, led by Mr. MacRae, the owner of a local store, were outraged by the use of profane language and by the sexual references. They demanded that the book be banned from use in Slippery Plains High School. However, another group of parents considered *Catcher in the Rye* to be a modern classic dealing with basic human problems and insisted that the book remain on the required reading list.

- Should *Catcher in the Rye* have been banned at the school?

- Should it remain on the required reading list? Or should its reading be optional, so that students whose parents oppose the use of the book would not read it and those whose parents approve of its use would read it?

- If Mr. MacRae's seventeen-year-old son, Harry, believed that he would not be affected adversely by the book and in fact would benefit from reading and discussing it in class, should he be allowed to read it?

- On what basis should we decide whether the discussion of a topic or the use of materials (e.g., books, films, records) is in "good taste": community standards; teacher's discretion; the view of the class (teacher and students); Department of Education regulations?

- If a book is considered very important by critics, professors, and other experts, yet is offensive to some people (even most people) in the community, would it be in good taste to teach it in the schools?

Teachers' beliefs

- Do Mrs. Gordon's radical views on social and political matters bring into question her suitability as a teacher? Do they make her better suited to teach than most? Or do these sorts of views not make a difference either way? If they do make a difference, specifically which views affect her suitability and *why* would they affect her suitability?

- Given her views, should Mrs. Gordon be permitted to teach anywhere in Saskatchewan? anywhere in Canada?

- Should teachers who don't condemn the use of drugs be permitted to teach in high schools? Should teachers advocating the use of drugs be permitted to teach in high schools?

- Should a teacher advocating racial discrimination and supporting Hitler's policies in the Second World War be permitted to teach young students?

- Should someone living in a communal marriage and not restricted to one wife/husband at a time be permitted to teach?

- Should a teacher dressing and living in "hippie-style" be permitted to teach?

- On what basis should we decide on whether a teacher's beliefs or life style make him unfit to teach students?

The inquiry

- In the Gordon case, were the members of the committee justified in holding a closed inquiry?

- Could Mrs. Gordon have gotten a fair hearing if the inquiry had been open?

- Was the Minister of Education justified in ordering the withdrawal of charges of gross misconduct against Mrs. Gordon?

- Should the decision on whether to reinstate Mrs. Gordon have been left to the school board? to the minister? to the committee? How would you defend your view?

- Can you suggest any fairer means of deciding whether Mrs. Gordon was to return to teaching in Moosomin?

Final consideration

- Is the probable end of Mrs. Gordon's teaching career to be seen as the unfortunate loss of a creative teacher or as the elimination of a teacher who failed to consider the standards and needs of her students and of the community?

THE CALGARY SEX EDUCATION CONTROVERSY

If there is any subject more controversial than religious education, it is sex education. Recent conflicts over this subject have created bitter divisions within communities across North America. Supporters see sex education as a means of producing an emotionally healthier, better balanced generation; opponents see it both as a plot to corrupt the young and as a violation of parental rights.

Early in 1968 the Calgary Board of Education commissioned two feasibility studies on the role of sex and family life education in the public and high schools of the city. Both studies recommended that such a program be integrated into the curriculum from kindergarten through high school with special seminars in sex at the high school level. Questions of family life would be examined whenever they naturally arose in such subjects as literature, science, and health.

Even before these studies were released there was growing controversy. Two organizations, the Society for the Prevention of Sex Education and the Citizens for Better Schools, were formed to oppose sex education, and page five of the *Calgary Herald* became the sounding board for concerned citizens. Critics of sex education saw in it a serious threat to parental rights and to the normal development of children. Supporters, including most church and community groups, saw sex education as an opportunity to produce better-rounded people. Articles as well as letters were published, and feelings ran high.

When a member of the board invited young people to attend the board meeting on March 18, opponents saw the action as part of a plot to force sex education on Calgary. After all, young people were not considered capable of making such a significant decision, even though at that meeting they pleaded for a "good clean source of information". Churches and the Pastoral Institute also presented briefs supporting the introduction of sex and family life education.

At the meeting of the board on April 29, a decision was finally made. Teachers would not be allowed to introduce matters regarding sex and family life but could give factual information if students raised questions; schools could set up special seminars at the junior high school level on sex information but these must be optional and after regular school hours.

An uneasy compromise had been reached. As one trustee said, "Everybody has won. The people who want sex and family life education can have it. They who don't want it don't have it."

The Issues

The voice of the people

Below are some of the issues raised and arguments presented by concerned citizens in the *Calgary Herald* at the height of the controversy over sex education. Where do you stand on these issues?

In a letter from "Happy As I Am" (April 26, 1969), a sixteen-year-old girl called for the abandonment of sex education in schools because it destroyed the innocence of the young children studying the subject and also because it led to the decay of our society. Rather than being forced on unprepared minds, matters of sex should be taken as they come.

- Do you agree that the study of sex would destroy the innocence of young children? Would it lead to the decay of our society? How can people know these kinds of things?
- Should matters of sex take their natural course or should one prepare oneself for future life by studying the subject first?
- Since girls have periods and boys may have wet dreams, which may upset them if they are uninformed, should they not be prepared by studying such matters?

According to Arland Reil (April 29, 1969) "sex is too holy, beautiful and sacred" to be treated in public education. To present the subject in a classroom would be to drag it down to "a common level".

- Do you agree that the teaching of sex would cheapen it?
- Is sex too important to have it publicly taught by virtual strangers?

It was contended by John R. Loome (March 26, 1969) that "The Anglo-Saxon hang-up on sex, which has dominated the North American culture for years, has resulted in a society which has more marriage failure, more adultery, more juvenile promiscuity, more broken homes, more violence, more psychotics and more unhappiness than any other society you could name. To come closer to home, Alberta has, I understand, one of the highest, if not the highest, illegitimacy rates per capita in Canada. And this despite all the sermonizing, Bible-belt preaching, keep the Sunday holy and down-with-demon-drink outlook of local officialdom. It hardly seems, therefore, that the existing system is working too well or that we could do much worse with formal sex education."

- Was Mr. Loome right in claiming that "the Anglo-Saxon hang-up on sex" is the cause of widespread marriage failure, adultery, unhappiness, juvenile promiscuity, violence, and psychosis? Is there such a hang-up? If so, is the lack of proper sex education the reason? What evidence do you have to support your belief?
- If ignorance about sex caused such things as marriage failure, would this be sufficient grounds for instituting a compulsory program of sex education?

Mr. Loome also made the following analogy: " . . . there are those who suggest that, in giving sex education, the school board is, or would be, usurping the rights of the parents. These people should consider an archaic law which existed, and may still exist, in many parts of the world. If a legal right-of-way existed across a private property, and the owner of that property prevented its use for one year and one day without protest, then the right-of-way no longer existed. In other words, a right that is not exercised may be abdicated. For many years, the vast majority of parents have not exercised their right to give children sex education."

- Do you agree that parents have lost their right to teach sex because in the past the vast majority of parents never exercised this right?
- If so, would this right automatically pass on to the government?

"A Student, Radical(?)" (March 13, 1969) argued against a program of sex education on the grounds that it denied to parents their right to decide which biases and which opinions were going to influence the minds of their children.

Along similar lines, Arland Reil (April 29, 1969) asserted that a parent can best judge when and under which conditions matters relating to sex should be discussed.

- Are parents most competent to teach sex?
- Is it their exclusive right?
- Is it their responsibility?

After high school students were invited to attend a Calgary School Board Committee meeting, "Very

Concerned Parent" (March 17, 1969) asked why students should be making decisions about sex education, since it is the taxpayers who vote the trustees into office and support the school system financially. He asked: "Are the students asked to make the decisions on whether they want to learn math, English, social studies, and so on? If children are able to make such a large decision, which may affect their whole lives – as too much sex education can be far, far more harmful than too little – why are they then not responsible for everything they do, and why are they kept within the family?"

- Do you agree with the writer that taxpayers, not students, should decide on which programs are best for students?

- Should non-taxpaying students have any say in programming? On what sorts of matters, if any, should they have a voice? Why?

- On matters "which may affect their whole lives", should students have the final say, or should taxpayers have this say? Can you suggest any better alternative for deciding these matters? Does the fact that neither students nor most parents are experts in matters of sex or education rule out either or both of these groups in deciding on matters affecting the students' "whole lives"?

On the other hand, "Student" (March 17, 1969) supported the development of the program, because, he argued, sex education "would allow for a healthier attitude toward sex. Sex would be taken from the gutter where it has been put by the ignorant."

- Do you agree that sex has been put in the gutter by the ignorant?
- Would teaching about sex improve or corrupt people's attitudes to sex? What evidence do you have to support your view?
- Since attitudes and feelings would be affected by sex education, should these matters be left to parents? to public education? to children to learn on their own or from friends?

It was argued by Reita Vance (April 29, 1969) that not even the biological aspects of sex should be taught, because such teaching would violate the parental right to teach morality to children. She wrote: "Certainly a parent has always had the right and privilege of teaching his culture, his beliefs and his religion to his offspring. . . . It is impossible to separate the moral aspects of sex education from the biological aspects. You omit the moral aspects entirely in an effort to minimize controversy, then you, in fact, are teaching that morals are not necessary or that they are not important. Why else should they be left out? . . . A teacher cannot teach a thing without revealing his or her own feelings and attitudes about that which he or she teaches. Feelings and attitudes come through to the students loud and clear."

- Can the biological aspects of sex (i.e., the physiology of sex) be taught apart from morality? What reasons do you have for taking your position?
- Is Reita Vance correct in asserting that the teacher's attitudes to sex would inevitably be revealed, and hence would influence the sexual

attitudes of his students? Can the teacher's feelings about sex be kept out?

- Should a teacher favouring "free love" be permitted to teach about sex in a biology course? in a health course?
- On the basis of your answers to the above questions, do you believe that the biological aspects of sex should or should not be taught?
- If it could be shown that sex education would decrease mental illness, the number of broken homes, and the divorce rate, should it be made compulsory for all despite parental objections that it is their right to teach their children morality and beliefs?
- Is it better to have competent teachers or uninformed parents teaching about sex?
- Is it better to have competent teachers or competent parents teaching about sex? Should there be sex education courses for parents?

"Concerned" (March 17, 1969) agreed with "Student", adding that sex ought to be taught because people are so interested in it. He wrote: "How to deal with their parents, their girl friend, their teacher and their society is far more dynamic to them than the out-dated history and science courses they are forced to take. What subjects are most adults discussing today? Sex, religion and politics. Yet every step in education has been away from the discussion or handling of these subjects within the school curriculum."

- Was "Concerned" right in arguing that the most-discussed subjects are those that *ought* to be taught in the schools? Is this always the case?

- Are those subjects that are rarely discussed (e.g., nuclear physics) not to be taught?
- On what basis should subjects studied in schools be chosen?

Public school trustee Harald Gunderson (February 26, 1969), a central figure in the controversy, criticized "so-called 'experts' telling parents they aren't competent to deal with this type of education".

Mr. Gunderson then went on to quote William McGrath, a Phoenix, Arizona, psychiatrist and critic of sex education in elementary schools: "Premature interest in sex is unnatural and will arrest or distort the development of the personality. Sex education should not be foisted on children; should not begin in the grade schools. . . ."

- Should the opinion of experts take precedence over the feelings and beliefs of parents in determining whether a sex education program should be presented?
- Can interest in sex ever be "unnatural"? Are there circumstances in which "the facts of life" should be hidden from children or even adults? If so, when and why?

The Calgary "solution"

In the end, the minority in Calgary opposing sex and family life education in the schools prevailed. Discussion of sexual matters could not be initiated by teachers in public schools, but teachers could answer factual questions raised by students. Seminars on sex education became extracurricular studies attended on a voluntary basis, and hence not part of the program.

- Was this a just solution of the conflict?
- Do experts have the right to impose their will on a minority in such deeply felt and explosive matters? Does the majority have the right to do so? Does the minority have the right *in these cases* of imposing its will on the majority? Would the same hold for the teaching of religion? Or do you see any difference in principle between them?

- Many of those opposed to sex education support religious education and vice versa. Are these people consistent? Can they have it both ways?

PARALLEL SITUATION. Anaheim, California, is the home of Disneyland. It is also, according to opponents of sex education, a playground of sex. A pamphlet called *Christianity and Sex* says: ". . . in Anaheim, Calif. venereal disease is out of control. Homes for unwed mothers are overcrowded and a marine replied, when asked why they crowd into Anaheim on weekends: Man, everybody knows the high school girls here are available." All of this is attributed to Anaheim's comprehensive sex and family life education program. Actually, the illegitimacy rate is one-third that of the state of California, there are no homes for unwed mothers in the county, and there is no evidence of an increase in the rate of venereal disease among high school students. It matters little. For many people in the

United States, "Sweden" and "Anaheim" are synonymous with "immorality".

There has always been some opposition to sex education in the public schools, but the forceful attack upon it from Watkins Glen, New York, to Wichita Falls, Texas, to San Marino, California, began with the publication of an article in the January 1969 issue of the *Bulletin* of the John Birch Society, which (in part) called for "organized, nationwide, intensive, *angry* and determined opposition to the now mushrooming program of so-called sex education in the public schools". The article went on to claim that sex education was ". . . from beginning to end, in execution and in purpose, simply a part of the overall Communist design".

The main target of this campaign was SIECUS (Sex Information and Education Council of the United States), its executive director Dr. Mary Calderone, and especially Dr. Isadore Rubin, editor of *Sexology* and one of fifty SIECUS board members. Dr. Rubin once refused to answer a congressional committee's questions concerning his possible Communist affiliations. SIECUS itself does not produce a program but acts as a clearing house for materials and encourages the development of programs and the initiation of sex education by the schools.

Within a year the campaign against SIECUS and sex education began to be successful. In twenty states the restriction or banning of sex instruction was considered and even Congress had to consider such a bill.

- What do you consider to be major issues in the foregoing case?

- In what ways is it similar to the Calgary sex education controversy? In what ways it is different?

The similarity between the American situation and that in Calgary is yet to be established. However, it is perhaps significant that the first major article published by the *Calgary Herald* on sex education reproduced all of the American arguments: the possibility that sex education was a part of a Communist conspiracy, the threat of SIECUS, and the necessity of setting sex in a religious context.

Beneath all of this rhetoric, beneath the claims of plot and counterplot, beneath the anger and fear and bitterness, a serious issue remains. Poll after poll has shown that a large majority of adults want sex education in the schools, and yet in town after town and district after district boards of education have been asked to abandon their family life programs because of vocal minority opposition.

- Can you suggest means of respecting both the will of the majority and the rights of the minority on the matter of sex education?

*The Calgary sex education controversy:
two years later*

Léo LaFrenière is a graduate of the Institute of Sexology and Family Science at the University of Louvain in Belgium. He is the first man in Canada to put together a course of family life studies from kindergarten to Grade 13. He was employed by the Thunder Bay Separate School Board and retained by the public school board to set up a sex education program. And one other thing – Léo LaFrenière is an Oblate priest, a Roman Catholic.

In June 1971 the Calgary Public School Board voted to appoint Father LaFrenière to the $14,000 a year post of preparing and instituting a family life and sex education program in the public schools.

Trustees Harald Gunderson and Deloy Sallenback called the appointment outrageous. They were concerned about the hiring of a man from outside the public school system, and particularly a man of a different religious persuasion from that of the students for whom the program was to be developed.

- Is it appropriate that Father LaFrenière, a priest belonging to a religion other than that of the majority of students, be appointed to devise and teach a program of family life and sex education? Would anyone belonging to a religion other than that of the majority of students be unsuitable to direct such a program? On what grounds would you support your position?
- Does the fact that he is a priest and unmarried limit his effectiveness as program designer and teacher?
- Could a priest be expected to treat without bias such family problems as "the new morality", contraception, and abortion?
- What would you consider fair treatment of these topics?
- Should an expert like Father LaFrenière be called upon to design and teach a program of family life and sex education, or should it be left to parents,

local doctors, and other trusted people in the community?

SOTTO. In September 1969 Mrs. Bruno Parisotto withdrew her daughter, Rebecca, from M. M. Robinson Secondary School in Halton County Public School System in Ontario. She protested against the teaching of sex education, which she called "vulgar and profane". She was especially incensed at the material available to students, notably a survey taken by teacher Ed Day asking students' opinions about sexual intercourse, masturbation, drugs, religion, and alcohol. On the questionnaire were questions asking whether the children had had sexual intercourse and whether they had masturbated. Although the family were Pentecostal adherents, Rebecca was subsequently enrolled in a private Catholic girls' school.

- If sex education is presented in a certain district should parents have a say as to what is presented? Should parents have to accept programs designed by experts in the field?
- Was it right for Mr. Day to ask such personal questions? Was it a violation of personal privacy? Now that the government has disclaimed any right to be in the bedrooms of the nation, have the public schools inherited the right to be there?
- Should students be permitted to exempt themselves from answering in such cases? Should they have this right regarding psychological tests that ask this sort of question? regarding IQ tests that are used

to organize classes according to ability? with regard to examinations?

- On what basis should we decide whether material is suitable or too private in the school setting?

PARALLEL SITUATION: THE CASE OF AUDREY MAEN-PAA. In the summer of 1971 Audrey Maenpaa, a fifteen-year-old Grade 11 student at Harbord Collegiate in Toronto, received a $785 provincial grant to establish a high school birth control campaign committee. The aims were: improved sex education courses in Metro high schools, mobile clinics providing birth control devices and abortion referrals for students, and family planning seminars in the schools.

- Was it right for a student to disseminate this material at a high school level? Would it be right for a teacher? Would it be right for a minister? Would it be right for any private individual? Would it be right for a doctor?
- Which of the following belong in the schools: sex education, provision of birth control devices, abortion referrals? On what principle would one decide which are to be allowed and which are not?
- Should public funds be used for these purposes? If so, should government funds also be provided for anti–birth control and anti-abortion materials?

II

POLITICS IN THE SCHOOLS

THE POLITICAL BELIEFS OF TEACHERS

When the War Measures Act was invoked in October 1970, few Canadians were unaffected by the drama of the events taking place. Rarely in Canadian history have the feelings of people right across the country run so high. Just as the supporters of the government action strongly believed that the W.M.A. was necessary in the crisis, so the critics of the government considered the W.M.A. to be unnecessary and dangerous. Thus, at the same time, there were calls for withdrawing the Act and calls for very strict application of the provisions of the Act.

Outside of Quebec, which was the scene of the drama, the conflict between the pro- and anti-government positions was deepest in British Columbia. One minor storm developed when Mr. Tom Campbell, Mayor of Vancouver, suggested that the War Measures Act be used to curtail the activities of dope pushers and other "undesirables". However, the mayor's opponents claimed that the wholesale use of extraordinary powers of arrest and detention would turn Canada into a police state.

It was in this highly charged setting, on October

21, 1970, that Arthur Norton Olsen, a teacher at South Peace Secondary School in Dawson Creek, British Columbia, was dismissed after expressing his political views on the crisis in Quebec. Earlier, a group of students in the school, after consulting with the principal, had decided to send a telegram to Ottawa expressing their support for the government stand in the crisis. When they approached Mr. Olsen for his signature, he expressed his reservations about their project. Mr. Olsen did not believe that the students were sufficiently informed on the situation to send a telegram in support of the government position.

After the encounter, a number of parents and students complained to the South Peace River school board that Mr. Olsen supported the Front de Libération du Québec. At a special meeting of the school board, the charges of the students were heard and Mr. Olsen was given the opportunity to reply. Although there was no total agreement between teacher and students as to what Mr. Olsen had said, the school board decided to dismiss him. No definite reason for dismissal was given, but one member of the board said that some of Mr. Olsen's remarks about the F.L.Q. may have been a factor. Another possible factor may have been that Mr. Olsen did not have a teacher's certificate.

According to Mr. Olsen, he had told the students that the federal government was wrong to invoke the War Measures Act in order to deal with the abductions of Mr. James Cross and Mr. Pierre Laporte. Mr. Olsen had further criticized the federal government for bringing troops into Quebec. He believed that the people of Quebec had a right to independence and that the government measures had denied them this basic right. He even said there was some similarity between the sending of federal troops into Quebec and the sending of Soviet troops into Czechoslovakia in 1968.

The next day, on October 22, 1970, the provincial Cabinet issued an order-in-council expressing the government's position on the right of school teachers to advocate certain political positions. The order states "as public policy of the province of British Columbia that no person teaching or instructing our youth in any educational system receiving public support should be in employment of that institution if he advocates the policies of the F.L.Q. or the overthrow of democratically elected governments by violent means."

On the basis of this order-in-council, Attorney General Leslie Peterson believed that schools and universities would dismiss teachers advocating "anti-democratic" revolutionary policies. Schools not carrying out the policy could be deprived of grants, although no explicit statement to this effect was made.

Mr. Peter Powell, President of the B.C. School Trustees Association, agreed with the attorney general. Because school boards were the agents of the government, they must conform to the orders issued. However, Mr. Powell did not believe that teachers would be prevented from studying the origin and policies of the F.L.Q. or from examining all sides of an issue fairly. The government order would simply mean that teachers advocating political violence would be excluded from the classroom.

However, not all individuals or groups supported the British Columbia government order-in-council. The B.C. Teachers' Federation, B.C. Bar Association, and B.C. Civil Liberties Association all took stands against the order. It was claimed that teachers were unfairly singled out in the order and that the order could be misused by boards against teachers. The most common complaint was that the language used was vague. Although the order stated that anyone who "advocates the policies of the F.L.Q." should not be employed in the educational system, the terms "policies" and "advocates" were nowhere defined. Because the wording was so vague, critics feared that no one would ever know who was violating government policy.

It was also reported that Federal Justice Minister John Turner had misgivings about the B.C. Cabinet action as well as about suggestions that emergency powers be used against such people as drug pushers. Mr. Turner was concerned that the actions taken by the B.C. government might be interpreted as use of the emergency powers granted under the W.M.A. The question is whether the order-in-council went beyond the terms and intent of the W.M.A.

However, Premier W.A.C. Bennett, Attorney General Peterson, and the other members of the Cabinet were confident that, despite the criticisms, their policy was clear and had very wide support in their province.

The Issues

- Should Arthur Norton Olsen have been dismissed from his teaching position for the stand he took during the 1970 crisis in Quebec?

Student involvement in political issues

- Were the students right in sending a telegram of support to the federal government for its action during the Quebec crisis?

- Should the students have also tried to get teachers' signatures for their telegram?

- Should the principal have given the students support in their sending of the telegram?

- Would the students have been equally justified if they had strongly condemned the government for its actions? Why?

- Is it appropriate for students in a public secondary school to engage in political activity? Should they be permitted: to form a United Nations Club; to support political refugees in the Biafran War; to form Liberal, Progressive Conservative, N.D.P., or Social Credit political clubs; to give support to a militant black or Indian power movement in their community?

The hearing

- Would the students and parents in Dawson Creek be justified in complaining to the school board against Mr. Olsen or any other teacher for either: questioning the wisdom of the students in sending the telegram in support of the federal government; opposing the invocation of the W.M.A.; criticizing the sending of federal troops into Quebec; comparing the federal government action with actions of the Soviet government; or doing all of the foregoing?

- Would making the remarks Mr. Olsen said he made justify the calling of a hearing of the school board?

- Do you believe that Mr. Olsen could have gotten a fair hearing by the school board in his community during the 1970 crisis in Quebec?

Dissent during national emergencies

- In times of emergency, should people in positions of responsibility and influence in society, regardless of their own personal views, be expected to give support to the actions of the democratically elected government dealing with the issue?

ANALOGY. During the Second World War, a member of Parliament opposed the conscription of troops on grounds of his personal belief about individual rights,

even though the majority of his constituents supported it and the government believed that it would
contribute to the war effort.
- Did he have the right to do so?
- Was it in the interests of Canada that he expressed
  his opposition to conscription?

The B.C. order-in-council

- Did the British Columbia Cabinet have the moral
  right to pass an order-in-council stating its policy
  towards teachers with certain radical views?

Subversives in education

- Is it just to exclude from teaching individuals supporting the F.L.Q. or advocating the violent overthrow of the Canadian government?

- If only people with "correct" views can teach,
  would it be likely or possible that the origin and
  policies of the F.L.Q. would be examined from all
  sides fairly?

- Is the order-in-council clear? Is the phrase "advocating the policies of the F.L.Q." clear? Is there
  danger that the order could be misused by officials
  misinterpreting the phrase?

THE BEILAN CASE. In the United States there have
been a number of widely discussed cases in which
teachers have been dismissed for membership in the
Communist party or for refusing to answer whether
they belong to the Communist party.

On November 18, 1953, Herman A. Beilan, a teacher in the Philadelphia public school system, was called to testify at a televised hearing of a sub-committee of the Committee on Un-American Activities of the U.S. House of Representatives. At these hearings the infiltration of members of the Communist party into the American educational system was being investigated.

Although Mr. Beilan denied being a member of the Communist party at the time and denied that he had ever advocated the violent overthrow of the government, he refused to answer questions about his past associations with this political group. Shortly thereafter, Mr. Beilan was informed by the Superintendent of Schools in the Philadelphia system that he was being dismissed as "unsatisfactory".

However, Mr. Beilan had been queried earlier by the Superintendent about his past Communist activities because his loyalty had come into question. On the advice of his counsel, he had refused to answer these questions; but no action was taken against him at the time, partly, it would appear, because his teaching abilities were considered satisfactory.

This changed when Mr. Beilan appeared on public television. The authorities then viewed the refusal to answer the questions as an admission of disloyalty. And since teachers had influence in shaping the beliefs and attitudes of young students, disloyalty made them unfit to teach in public schools.

- Should a person in a position of trust and responsibility who refuses to answer questions about past radical political activities be permitted to continue in that position?

- Is refusal to answer such questions a very strong suggestion of guilt?
- Should admitted Communists calling for the violent overthrow of democratic governments be permitted to teach in high schools?
- Are such people necessarily unfit to teach? Why?

PARALLEL SITUATION. In New York City a subway conductor for the New York Transit System was dismissed under the Security Risk Law. As in the Beilan case, the conductor refused to tell a superior whether he was a member of the Communist party. This refusal was considered evidence that the conductor was neither trustworthy nor reliable. As a result he was judged unfit to be a conductor in the public employment.

- Are Communist conductors unfit to operate subways in the United States? in Canada?
- When do the beliefs of individuals in society make them security risks?
- Does the government have the right to refuse employment to people belonging to subversive organizations regardless of the work involved?

PARALLEL SITUATION. Steps have been taken to prevent use of what have been considered subversive books and other materials in public educational institutions. In 1959 one representative to the Florida state legislature proposed a bill to ban books written by known Communists or by people who refuse to answer whether they were connected to subversive political groups. He also proposed a ban on all books that presented any other political system as superior to the American system of democratic government and free enterprise. After a long debate, the bill was rejected, but the legislature did go on record as opposing the use of texts that presented any non-American policial approach as superior to the American system.

- Should the government decide which materials public schools can or cannot use?
- Should it have the right to ban all books written by known Communists or members of subversive groups?
- Which of the following types of books, if any, should the government ban if written by persons with anti-democratic beliefs: books on guerrilla warfare and the manufacture of explosives; books on citizenship and politics; history books; novels and plays; geometry books?
- Should governments rule that materials questioning the superiority of their economic and political systems be kept out of school?
- Could not such materials adversely affect or influence the though of impressionable young people?

Research activities

- On the basis of public opinion polls and your own research and experience, do most Canadians support the order-in-council of the British Columbia Cabinet?
- Investigate the relevant provisions in the War Measures Act for this case. Did the order-in-council of the British Columbia Cabinet go beyond these provisions?

PEACE CLUB*

City Health Inspector Martin Moritz was on a routine tour of the facilities at Parkhurst Collegiate when he spotted a poster in the girls' locker room.

"Stop the Killing Now!" it read. At the bottom was the name of the group who had sponsored it – the Students' Committee to End the War in Vietnam.

Moritz, a refugee from Eastern Europe and an active member of the anti-Communist Edmund Burke Society, was horrified! "This is nothing less than Communist brainwashing," he complained to Principal Walter Blake. "Young and impressionable minds are being perverted by one-sided Red propaganda!"

Blake agreed that Parkhurst students should hear both sides of any social issue, but refused to ban posters put up by members of the school's Peace Club. "The Peace Club is a legitimate school organization," he told the inspector. "So far as I know, it is not run by Communists; and I do not intend to stop it from advertising."

Moritz went storming out of the principal's office,

*Based on an incident at a Metro Toronto high school.

48

certain that Blake was in collusion with Communist students. On a bulletin board at the main entrance to the school, he found another poster announcing a Peace Club meeting. It carried the international "Ban the Bomb" insignia. Mr. Moritz was now absolutely convinced that Communists were behind the organization.

Moritz set out on a campaign for public support to fight the Peace Club. He sent letters to the school board, the newspapers, and radio and television stations throughout the area. Before long, phone calls from concerned parents were pouring into Principal Blake's office.

Finally the school board decided to hold a hearing on the matter, to determine if Peace Club members had overstepped their right to advocate social causes. In the meantime, the Edmund Burke Society was invited to hold meetings on school grounds. Posters quickly appeared urging students to come to the society's meetings to learn the truth about Communism and Communist propaganda, but the turnout was poor.

A week later, at the school board hearing, Peace Club President Mitchell Vickers, an American draft-dodger, testified that the club had sponsored film showings about the Vietnam War – with one film made by the U.S. Information Agency, the other by the government of North Vietnam. He said that the organization's main purpose was to stimulate discussion of the issues with a view toward promoting universal peace among men.

Mr. Moritz then asked Principal Blake to explain

his approval of the Peace Club's activities. Moritz charged that the club was a breeding ground for radicals and that these activists carried their bad behaviour out into the community. Blake replied that the Peace Club was a popular and well-organized group that fostered intelligent discussion on important public issues. He pointed out that the club's popularity was a credit to the fine leadership of its president, and that to his knowledge the club's activities had never caused a disturbance in the school. Vickers admitted that many members had participated in peace marches. "That's the whole point, isn't it?" he asked. "To be involved, to form an intelligent opinion on political issues . . . then to act on that opinion."

Parent observers at the hearing also spoke up. Some opposed the display of such posters on school property, while others expressed support for Mr. Blake's position and for the aims of the Peace Club.

Members of the Edmund Burke Society also present at the hearing were not impressed by the principal's arguments. "This is still brainwashing," one of them insisted. "We have lived under Communism; we know it for what it is, for what it does to the individual. We cannot stand by in silence while Communist propaganda is being displayed in our school!"

There seemed little chance for a solution that would satisfy everyone. After hearing arguments on both sides, the trustees met in closed session to decide what should be done about the Peace Club.

The Issues

- What decision should the school board make about the Peace Club? How would you justify this decision, if you were a trustee?

- Was Mr. Moritz justified in complaining about the students' extracurricular activities to the principal? to the board? to the newspapers and radio stations? Who should decide what extracurricular activities take place in the school?

A Toronto Board of Education ruling says, "All teachers shall refrain from discussing in the schools questions purely political or ecclesiastical or theological and from expressing anywhere opinions adverse to British institutions or sentiments disloyal to the Crown."

- Do you support or oppose this regulation? Why?

- Who decides what is taught in your school? Who do you think should decide? The Hall Dennis Report makes 258 recommendations for high schools in Ontario. None of these recommendations suggests that students be given the power to determine the curriculum or participate in its development. Should students be included in curriculum planning activities? Why or why not?

- Should the community have a voice in what is being taught in the school? If there is a conflict between the community and the school authorities over what is to be taught, how should the conflict be resolved? Should the school expose students to ideas, attitudes, and values that the community does not share?

At Parkhurst Collegiate, a year after the Peace Club incident, the principal received a complaint from Mrs. J., a parent who discovered that the school library had a subscription to the *Peking Review,* published in China. Mrs. J. felt that this exposure to Communist thought was dangerous to students and would make them susceptible to Communist propaganda. She threatened to complain to the board and to the newspapers if the magazine were not immediately withdrawn from the library shelves. The principal withdrew the magazine because he did not want more adverse publicity.

- Was Mrs. J. right to pressure the principal in this way?
- If the principal had refused her demand and she went to the newspapers, should they give widespread publicity to her complaint?
- Should students have access to reading material containing political views radically different from those accepted by the majority of people in the community?

At the same time, in a public library in the city, a group of parents called on the librarian and asked her to remove *Little Black Sambo* from the children's section of the library because they claimed the book downgraded black people and fostered racial prejudice.

- Should the librarian remove the book? Are the parents justified in their request? Do you agree or disagree with their criticism of the book?
- How does this situation differ from the one directly above? How are they alike?
- Who should decide what reading material should be made available to young children and older students: their parents; teachers; prominent members of the community; psychologists, reading specialists, or other experts; the children or students themselves?

- Should schools operate as free and open market places of ideas? Are some ideas or topics too controversial or dangerous to be read or talked about in school? If you were a parent, would you be in favour of or opposed to the following ideas or topics being discussed by your children in high school: the philosophy and policies of the F.L.Q.; the philosophy and policies of the Communist party of Canada; birth control methods; homosexuality; unusual religious customs and practices in Canada; arguments in favour of racial separation based on "evidence" of racial inferiority; arguments of a group advocating expulsion of all Americans from Canada; discussions concerning the nature and existence of God and an "afterlife"? Why?

DISCUSSION OF VIETNAM

Thursday, November 13, 1969. The Vietnam Mobilization Committee and Students Against the War in Vietnam sent a group led by spokesman Joe Young to the Toronto Board of Education with the proposal that special school assemblies be organized by high school principals, teachers, and students to discuss the war in Vietnam.

Chairman Alex Thompson expressed the opinion that this proposal was not the sort of matter the board could decide on. However, the board agreed to hear the proposal since, as trustee Mahlon Beach said, "If we don't give them a chance to be heard we're giving them an opportunity to say that we are trying to muzzle expression of thought." Mr. Beach went on to ask whether the group making the proposal was a Communist-front organization.

Mr. Young began by saying that he was pleased that the board chairman had reconsidered and was willing to have the board listen to the group. However, Trustee William Lang objected to what he considered to be an implicit criticism of the chairman of the board, although he did agree to listen to the proposal.

Mr. Young then made his proposal and the chairman asked for questions. "I have a number of questions," began Mr. Beach. "First one: is this a Communist-front organization?"

Mr. Young denied Communist association in an indirect manner.

"Were you born in Canada, Mr. Young?"

"That's an irrelevant question."

"Then, I assume you were not born in Canada. . . . You are too young to be a war veteran. Are you married?"

Next Trustee Ernest Jones began his attack on the group and its submission to the board. He objected to the board's permitting the proposal to be presented at all. He then went on to note that there are many veterans in Canada who fought in the Second World War for democracy and for the rights of people like those in the group. Besides, he claimed, it was outside the jurisdiction of the Toronto Board of Education to interfere with the war in Vietnam.

At this point, other trustees criticized Mr. Beach for his irrelevance and Mr. Jones for his inevitable reference to Second World War veterans. In the end the board decided that they could not deal with the proposal; it was a matter for school principals.

The Issues

- Should there be any political discussion in the publicly supported high schools? If so, which of the following would you consider to be legitimate, and which illegitimate: discussion of the Canadian political systems; discussion of which Canadian political party is the best; discussions of the war in Vietnam; taking positions on the F.L.Q's political platform?

- Should the Board of Education hear representations of student proposals such as this one for the formation of assemblies to discuss the Vietnam War?

PARALLEL SITUATION: THE VIETNAM SIT-IN. Six months later, a group of students led by Barry Weisleder, seventeen-year-old president of the Student Council of Sir Sanford Fleming Secondary School, appeared at a meeting of the North York Board of Education. They demanded that their brief, proposing that assemblies to discuss the war in Vietnam be held in the high schools, be heard.

After consultation, the board decided first to discuss whether they could hear the brief, since their policy was to refuse to listen to student delegations. The discussion of this item lasted for several hours. Then, at 12:15 a.m., the student group demanded that its brief be heard and refused to acknowledge calls to order. Board Chairman Lynn Trainor declared the meeting closed, but some students remained.

Eventually a police sergeant and a constable were required to escort Mr. Weisleder from the board room, after which the other twenty or so students left voluntarily.

- Should students be permitted to present briefs to boards of education?
- Are students justified in using sit-in tactics in order to be heard or to achieve their aims?
- Is a Communist-led group to be given the same consideration when presenting a proposal as a group supporting our democratic system?
- Does discussion of the Vietnam War constitute interference with that war?
- Should the Board of Education be able to decide on whether the war in Vietnam can be discussed in the schools? Should they be able to decide whether or not a rally against the war in Vietnam can be held in the schools?

III

RELIGION AND EDUCATION

THE CASE OF PAUL PETERSON*

"I don't believe that Jesus fed all those people like it said in the story you read before supper!" said Paul, the oldest of the three Peterson children.

"Of course He did, Paul. The Bible tells us He did. Who has been telling you that?" asked Mr. Peterson.

"Well, Mr. McBride, you know the minister who teaches us religion, he told us the same story just Friday but he told it differently."

"How did he tell it?"

"He said that when people saw how kind Jesus and the disciples were, sharing their tiny bit of food, they got out things they had brought along and shared them too, so that when everybody shared, there was enough for everybody. He says that's one of the great things Jesus teaches us – to be kind and to share."

"Paul," Mr. Peterson tried to hold his temper. "You know that the Bible says more than that. It says that Jesus performed a miracle – He made five loaves and

*This story is based on an incident mentioned in the "Brief of the Diocese of Huron of the Anglican Church of Canada to the Committee on Religious Education in the Public Schools of Ontario".

two fishes enough food for five thousand people. That's what the Bible says and that's what we believe. 'And they all ate and were satisfied. And they took up twelve baskets full of broken pieces and of the fish. And those who ate were five thousand men.' " Mr. Peterson closed the family Bible. "To believe anything else is to deny our faith. Jesus was more than just another good man. You do understand that, don't you, Paul?"

"Yes, but Mr. McBride . . ."

Mr. Peterson had worried about his son all day. What was the school system doing to him? It seemed that the faith the Petersons had worked so hard to implant in their children was being undermined.

As soon as he got home, his wife told him about her attempts to straighten the problem out. First she had called the principal. He said that he had no previous complaints about Mr. McBride, who was an Anglican Minister and taught two classes of Grade 7 children. While he was sympathetic, he could not see that the use of a Bible story to point up a moral truth might be objectionable. However, he did suggest that if the Petersons were deeply concerned they might have Paul exempted from the classes. Since these classes were held during the last period in the afternoon on Friday, he could be allowed to go home early. Mrs. Peterson got no further in her call to Mr. McBride, who could not see how he could have offended anyone. He had gone out of his way to reduce the Gospel to its common denominator and surely the Gospel was the basis of morality.

"The only thing we can do", Mr. Peterson said after some thought, "is have him exempted."

"I talked to Paul after school," Mrs. Peterson said. "He wants to stay in the class. He says he'd be the only one to leave and he'd feel embarrassed. Even David Katz, who is a Jew, stays for the class."

"That's too bad," Mr. Peterson replied. "But it is better that he should be embarrassed than to have his faith undermined. You call the principal tomorrow and make the arrangements."

The Issues

- Should Mr. Peterson have had his son Paul exempted from classes in religion even though it would cause embarrassment to Paul? Why?

- Should subjects that some parents and students find morally or religiously unacceptable be taught in public schools? Why?

The teaching of religion

- Was it right to have a minister of a specific denomination conduct classes on religious subjects in a public school comprised of students of different religious denominations, as in the Peterson case? Present reasons in support of your position.

- If every student in the school had been from an Anglican background, would it have been justified to have an Anglican minister teach religion there? If eighty per cent were Anglican, would it then have been justified? If ten per cent were Anglican and the rest Roman Catholics and Jews, would it have been justified?

- Was the principal justified in supporting Reverend McBride's teaching of religion?

- Was it not reasonable to continue teaching a subject as long as there were no previous complaints?

- Can you think of any alternative open to the principal other than to say that Paul Peterson could ask for exemption from classes on religion? If you had been the principal, what would you have done in this situation, and why?

Alternative

- It has been suggested that all religious education be limited to optional classes taught after regular school hours. Would this be preferable to teaching religion during regular school hours in regular classes? Why? Would this have solved the problem in Paul Peterson's school?

- Do you think that it would be justifiable to use public facilities for the teaching of specific religious viewpoints?

- Should the teaching of any religion whatsoever be prohibited? Can religion be avoided in education? On what grounds would you justify your position?

- For which of the following should clergymen be permitted to take part in school programs: to lead prayers every day; to lead prayers on Remembrance Day; to teach a course on world religions; to teach a course on Greek mythology; to teach a course in English literature; to teach a course in physics?

Religious exercises

- Is it right to have religious exercises (i.e., hymns and prayers) in public schools?

- It has been argued that, since prayers are part of state occasions such as the opening of legislatures, participation in non-sectarian public prayers is good training for citizenship. Do you agree with this view? Is the argument convincing?

- Should the schools teach everything that is part of life? Where would you draw the line?

- Should religion and the state be totally separated? *Can* they be totally separated?

Religion and morality

- Is one goal of education to teach the difference between right and wrong, good and evil? If so, can this be done without actually teaching some religion? If not, would you ban all stories, including "The Three Pigs", that teach a lesson or have a moral?

- Should stories from the Bible (e.g., Noah and the ark, Sodom and Gomorrah, Jesus curing lepers, Jesus driving money-lenders from the Temple) be used to illustrate moral lessons in public school classes?

- Which of the following should or should not be used to illustrate moral lessons in public schools: Greek mythology; the lessons of Buddha; the Koran; *Macbeth; Catcher in the Rye; The Valley of the Dolls* or *Myra Breckenridge;* any book you consider to be obscene? Give reasons for your answer.

- It is suggested in the Mackay Report (see below, pp. 99-101) that moral education be integrated as far as possible with all subjects in the school program. Do you believe that moral lessons should be drawn from science? Can they be drawn from science?

- Should science be taught for any purpose other than to describe "the way the world is"? If so, what purpose should it serve: to tell us what is "normal" in sexual behaviour, social attitudes, and religious beliefs; to tell us which groups are superior to others; to help us discover how to win wars, or control population size?

Science and religion

- Should science be taught if its theories are in disagreement with what is stated in the Bible?

- Should the Bible be taught if its contents conflict with the findings of science? On what basis would you decide which is to be studied?

THE SCOPES MONKEY TRIAL. For eleven days in July 1925, Dayton, Tennessee, was the site of one of the best-known legal cases of the twentieth century. John Scopes, a high school biology teacher, had formally violated a law passed earlier that year that made it unlawful "to teach any theory that denies the story of the divine creation of man as taught in the Bible, and to teach instead that man has descended from a lower order of animals". This anti-evolution law had been passed by an overwhelming majority (95-11) in the state legislature.

The prosecution in the Scopes trial was assisted by William Jennings Bryan, an internationally known lawyer and politician and former presidential candidate. Among the defence lawyers were Clarence Darrow, the most famous criminal lawyer of his time, and other civil liberties lawyers of national repute. The judge ruled that questions as to both the constitutionality of the law and the validity of the theory of evolution were irrelevant. The only relevant issue was whether Scopes had taught evolution, and the defence admitted that he had. Scopes was found guilty and fined one hundred dollars. In 1927 the state supreme court upheld the constitutionality of the law but cleared Scopes on a technicality, thus heading off a test of its constitutionality in the U.S. Supreme Court.

- Was Scopes wrong on legal grounds? on moral grounds?
- The judge ruled that the validity of the theory of evolution was irrelevant. Should the validity of a theory ever be irrelevant where one is prosecuted for advocating that theory?
- Was the law a just law?
- Is there a place for teaching "the story of the divine creation of man" in a non-sectarian public school system?
- Is there a place for teaching the theory of evolution as scientific truth in science classes?
- Does the belief in divine creation conflict with the

belief in evolution? If they conflict, should the religious position alone be taught without the teacher's opinion?

In the U.S.S.R., the teaching of religious beliefs (except to one's own children) is prohibited by law. The reason usually given is that it prevents people from accepting the truths of science. As a result, the Biblical story of Jonah and the "big fish", in which Jonah was swallowed by a whale and remained inside it for three days without being digested, could not be told. Similarly, sympathetic treatment of other miracles, such as Joshua and the walls of Jericho, the miracle of the loaves and fishes, and the appearance of the Virgin Mary in Fatima, Portugal, on May 13, 1917, would be forbidden.

- Should those religious stories that conflict with scientific belief be taught as truth?
- Should they be taught as myth? as parable?
- Should they be taught "neutrally", neither as truth nor as fiction? Can this be done?
- Is there ever a real conflict between scientific and religious teachings? If so, how can it be resolved? If not, why is it *not* a *real* conflict?

Rights of parents and students

- Were the rights of Paul Peterson violated by Mr. McBride's teaching of the miracle of the loaves?

- Were the rights of David Katz, the Jewish boy in Paul Peterson's class, violated?

- Were the rights of students whose parents were non-believers violated?

- Were the rights of all students, regardless of belief, who did not request these classes violated? Why?

- Were the rights of Mr. and Mrs. Peterson violated by the teaching of this class? Why?

- Do you believe that it is the right of the Petersons to choose the form of religious education that their children are to have? Or is it the right of the government to decide which religious beliefs are to be taught in the schools? How would you support your position?

- Should the parents or the government determine which moral values are to be taught in public schools?

- Should students have a choice in this matter? If so, when? Is it right for you to be discussing this problem in school?

PARALLEL SITUATION. Christian Scientists believe that there is no such thing as physical illness and that what we call "illness" is basically "wrong thinking". If one believes that he is "ill", his cure can only be brought about by correct thoughts about God. After all, it is claimed, only spirit is real and spirit cannot have genuine physical disease. Therefore, all cures must be spiritual and come through the spirit from God.

- Should the children of the followers of the Christian Science belief be exempt from health classes discussing physical illness? from first aid classes? from biology classes? from physics classes?
- What rights should parents have in determining which subjects their children are to study? Why?

- If parents were opposed to the teaching of "new math", should their children be taught traditional mathematics? If the parents opposing "new math" were professional mathematicians with a world-wide reputation, should their children be exempt from studying the subject?
- If parents are opposed to dancing and have very strict beliefs about personal modesty, should their children be exempt from taking physical education classes, which include dancing?
- If parents believe that the earth is flat, should their children be exempt from science courses that include the study of the solar system?

Summary questions

- On what basis would you decide whether a subject dealing with factual content, religious content, or moral content is to be compulsory in the school program?

- On what basis would you decide whether it should be permitted in the program?

- What role are the teachers, parents, students, and government to have in deciding on these matters? Why?

Analogy: minority rights

When ten families formed a farming community north of Edmonton, Alberta, they all agreed to conduct communal affairs along strictly democratic lines. This meant that in all matters of general concern final decisions were to be made by majority vote.

One of the major tasks of the group was the setting up of an educational system that suited the needs of both the community and the individuals in the community. Among the subjects presented in the school was a practical course on home economics. Some members of the community felt that this was one of the most important subjects in the program because it related directly to many of the daily practical matters in their lives.

In this course, students first dealt with the nature of the foods they commonly consumed, and then actually prepared some of the foods. When one group came to the study and preparation of beef, one set of parents objected. They were vegetarians and opposed the killing, cooking, and consuming of animals. They insisted not only that their children be exempt from these studies, but also that the topic not be dealt with in the school.

A general meeting attended by all members of the community was held and the issues were discussed at length. At the conclusion of the discussion, several votes were taken. By a vote of eighteen to two it was decided that the course of study would be retained in the school. By sixteen to four it was decided that lessons on the nature of edible meats would still be given. And by thirteen to seven it was decided that classes in which meats were prepared were to be continued. It was unanimously agreed that no one would be forced to eat any food he or she prepared. The meeting was then adjourned.

- Should the lessons on the nature of edible meats have been compulsory for the children who were vegetarians? Why?
- Should vegetarians have been required to participate in the preparation of the meats?
- If two or three of the parents found the course to be offensive on moral grounds, should it be removed from the program?
- In matters of education does the majority ever have the right to impose its will on the minority? If so, when and why?
- In these matters does the minority ever have the right to impose its will on the majority? If so, when and why?
- If experts in the field of education are in the minority, should their views on school programs prevail?
- What alternatives are open to the vegetarians, once the decisions have been made? What would you have done in their place?
- Would the teaching of the nature of edible meats be like teaching about religion in the schools? Would you support the teaching of both, neither, or one of these?
- Would the preparation of meats in the Alberta community school be like having prayers or singing hymns in school classes? Are they different in any significant ways? Would you support both practices, neither, or one of the practices? On what basis would you support your position?

THE CASE OF
GERTRUDE CONRAD*

By the time her daughter, Debbie, had been in kindergarten for two months, Gertrude Conrad realized that
Debbie had rejected her family's ideas about religion.
Mrs. Conrad could only hope that it would be
temporary.

From the start there had been conflict between what
the teacher said and did and what the Conrads believed. While observing the class on the very first day,
Mrs. Conrad was surprised to hear the teacher lead
the children "Jesus Loves the Little Children". The
teacher remarked that she was certain they would all
know the hymn from Sunday School.

In mid September Mrs. Conrad attended a parent-
teacher's meeting and again was surprised when the
kindergarten teacher suggested that parents make
certain that their children attend Sunday School. She
noticed that about half of the books displayed in the
room were religious in nature, such as stories of
Jesus' life as a child and books of children's prayers.

---

*Names and places have been changed in deference to the
wishes of the people involved in this case.

Later Debbie told her mother that the teacher had said Jesus was a little boy just like her. Mrs. Conrad tried to explain to her daughter her own ideas about Jesus. She told her that Jesus was a very special person who lived a long time ago and who is remembered because he taught people to love one another.

The children were taught to say grace together before their milk and cookies, and the teacher also suggested that they should say grace before they ate at home. Mrs. Conrad did not believe in this type of prayer and did not want it taught to her children.

One week later Debbie told her that the teacher had said that God made the flowers and vegetables grow in the fields and the baby animals grow in their mommies' tummies. Mrs. Conrad tried to explain that some people considered nature to be God. She illustrated this view by referring to the seeds her daughter had planted in the spring and the way they had grown. Then she went on to explain her own view of God as all the good ideas people have that make them feel happy.

Because of this latest incident, Mrs. Conrad found the situation intolerable and spoke to the principal. The principal could not see that any religious indoctrination was taking place and refused to interfere with the teacher, but she did inform Mrs. Conrad that she could speak to the inspector.

A short time later Mrs. Conrad met with the inspector and the principal. The inspector said that, in his opinion, Department of Education regulations gave full authority to the teacher's actions. He suggested that Mrs. Conrad could voice her disapproval either by court action or by getting onto relevant committees.

By the end of October Debbie had stopped telling her parents about her teacher's comments on religion, and Mrs. Conrad realized that her daughter had decided to accept her teacher's opinion on religious matters.

The Issues

- Were the parental rights of Gertrude Conrad to teach her religious beliefs to her daughter violated by the religious practices in the school?

- Should Debbie Conrad have been excused from the religious activities of her class? Would this have been sufficient to solve the problem?

- In a kindergarten setting is it possible to exempt one child from a group activity?

- Is it wrong to have all the children in a kindergarten class sing hymns; listen to Biblical stories; say prayers; learn religious values? Would you agree to such exercises if everyone in the class had parental consent? if nearly all had parental consent? if no one had parental consent?

- Who has the right to teach religion: parents; the church; the school; no one?

- Should Mrs. Conrad take court action in order to eliminate religion from the classroom? Why?

- Should religious exercises be performed in senior high school? Who, if anyone, should be exempt from these?

ANALOGY. A Canadian diplomat and his family are posted at an outlying province in the U.S.S.R. The only school is a state school carrying out a vigorous anti-religious program. Several Russian parents in the area have objected to the program but their children have been required to participate in "Citizenship Education". The Canadian diplomat does not want to be separated from his young children but is unhappy with the program.

- Should he send his children to the state school if they are required to participate in that program?
- Should his children, as outsiders, be exempt from the program?
- Should religious members of the community be allowed to keep their children out of the program?

- Should the opening of Parliament include a brief non-sectarian prayer? In which public institutions is it appropriate to sing hymns and say prayers, and in which is it inappropriate?

Teacher *A* tell his class that nature can only be understood if we recognize the working of a higher religious force in the universe. Teacher *B* tells his class that science alone enables man to understand the universe he lives in.

- Has either teacher violated the rights of his students?
- Has either teacher violated the rights of the parents of his students? How?

SEPARATE SCHOOLS –
MANITOBA'S TICKING
TIME-BOMB*

When the Manitoba Royal Commission on Education issued its report a few months ago, it dropped a time-bomb that could blow the province into a bitter political and religious feud. The commission recommended separate schools for Manitoba.

"Wounds have been opened," a high Winnipeg education official said last week. He was right.

The wounds go back to 1890 when the Manitoba legislature abolished separate schools for Roman Catholics. Thus erupted the "Manitoba School Question", the greatest furore over schools in the history of Canada.

In the province, religious, political and educational factions flared. The act was appealed to the courts and went as far as the Privy Council in London, which upheld it. In Ottawa the Conservatives, in power since Confederation, fell into discord over the question. Prime ministers changed but eventually the government toppled (1896) and the Liberals under Laurier came to power. Although he was a Roman Catholic, Laurier sided with the abolitionists and

---

*By Thomas Allen, reprinted with permission from the Toronto *Daily Star,* June 1, 1961.

worked out an agreement. The question seemed to be settled for all time, and in the last 50 years has not been a live issue. Until now.

Now the bombshell.

Why did the commission recommend separate schools?

"Why did the MacFarlane commission do it? He's a historian. He should have known better", muttered another senior educational official. (The issue is so touchy that few allow themselves to be quoted by name.) Dr. R. O. MacFarlane, who headed the commission, is a former Manitoba history professor and deputy minister of education; he is now at Carleton University, Ottawa.

The commission's argument, concurred to by all five members including the Rev. Brother J. H. Bruns, is that other provinces have separate schools, that substantial religious minorities ought to have a right to schooling (for which they pay taxes) that meets their aspirations; that many now operate private schools and so have to pay double – the tax for public schools, the fees and Church levies for the parochial school.

The commission also argues that if separate schools existed, the public schools might benefit. This would be particularly true in areas where large religious minorities tend to give their schools a sectarian slant, even though they are public.

The commission has recommended what it calls "some measure of public support for private and parochial schools, without injuring the public school system". In its detailed financial recommendations for this, the suggested support is on a par with what the public schools receive from local taxes and government grants.

The proposed support would be given to approved separate schools whether Roman Catholic, Hutterite, Mennonite, Jewish, or even posh boarding schools for boys like Ravenscourt in Winnipeg. The existence of such schools gives educational variety, the commission said, suggesting that they be under a minimum of government supervision.

What has happened to this recommendation? Politicians are stalling on it.

Conservative Premier Duff Roblin, a Roman Catholic, has sidestepped the issue, even though taunted by former Liberal leader D. L. Campbell to declare himself. The Liberals have not taken a stand. Nor have the C.C.F., although their leader, Gildas Molgat, has publicly said he personally is opposed to establishing separate schools.

There the matter rests uneasily. But there are strong currents that will not let it rest long.

[This article by Thomas Allen has proven to be prophetic. In 1971 the separate school issue erupted again, splitting the cabinet of the N.D.P. government in Manitoba. Premier Ed Schreyer, a Roman Catholic, tried to reopen discussion of the issue of aid to separate schools, which he personally supported. However, a majority of his cabinet opposed this. Finally on March 2, 1972, the deep division within the government was manifested in the resignation of Minister of Mines and Resources Sidney Green over this issue. Many today believe that the fate of the new N.D.P. government hinges on its handling of this explosive problem.]

The Issues

- Do you believe that your province should have a single educational system for all students, or should it be divided along religious lines if various groups want it so? How would you justify your position?

- If you agree in principle with the existence of parochial or separate schools, do you think that the government should undertake to set up and finance such schools, or should each religious group set up its own system?

Minority rights

- Given the fact that a sizeable minority of citizens wanted a separate Roman Catholic system of education, was the Manitoba Royal Commission on Education justified in recommending support for such a system?

- Do you agree with the commission that religious minorities paying school taxes have a right to schooling "which meets their aspirations"?

- How large should a minority be before it has schooling rights?

ANALOGIES. Consider whether taxpaying minorities have rights to determine government programs in the following cases:

- A community of Indians in an isolated region of northern Manitoba insist that they have a right to roads and electricity, despite the high cost to the government. Would it weaken their case if none of the members of the community paid taxes? Should taxpayers have privileges non-taxpayers do not have?

- A group of citizens interested in Beethoven, Rembrandt, and Shakespeare demand that the publicly owned Canadian Broadcasting Corporation set aside prime time to present programs in which they are interested. Even though no more than five per cent of television viewers will watch these programs, the citizens consider it their right as taxpayers and members of society. Do you agree? On what grounds?

- Could groups interested in witchcraft or umbrella designing make similar claims that you would support? Where would you draw the line? Why?

Financial consideration

- Was the Manitoba Royal Commission on Education right in recommending that parochial or religious schools receive their share of government grants?

- Is it right that separate school supporters pay double for the privilege of having their own schools?

- Should people who send their children to private schools receive government financial support? Should they pay double for the privilege?

Unity or diversity in education?

- Does the existence of separate school systems affect the unity of the country in any way? What evidence do you consider relevant to the issue?

- Do you think that a variety of school systems is desirable in our society? Does it help enrich the community educationally?

- Was the Manitoba commission justified in disturbing the unified school system in 1960 in order to give minority groups of taxpayers their right to schooling of their choice?

- Would it not be fair if each community decided on its own system of schooling and its own programming? In a district which is predominantly Mennonite, should not the major system be determined by Mennonites?

Research question

- Investigate the background to and the issues raised in the "Manitoba Schools Question" of 1890 and the split in the Manitoba cabinet 1971-2.

The voucher system

It has been suggested by leading educators, politicians, and economists in Britain, the United States, and Canada that the only fair means of educational support is "the voucher system". Under this system, every student attending schools would be granted a voucher sufficient to cover the costs of his education

for a given period. The student could then choose
to attend any school in the province that would
accept him, be it a public, secular, or non-secular
private school. In other words, there would be a
competitive or free-enterprise system of education
in the province. Those schools that did not attract
a sufficient number of students to cover their oper-
ating costs would cease to operate. According to the
supporters of the system, only those schools serving
the needs or wishes of a sufficient number of students
could survive.

- Do you think the "voucher system" would resolve
  the inequalities of our present system?
- Would it disrupt the stability of our present
  system?
- Is the disruption that may result worth the benefits
  that may be derived?

The non-issue

When Premier William Davis of Ontario refused to
extend aid past Grade 10 for separate schools, he
expressed the hope that it would not become an
issue in the 1971 provincial election. Opposition
leaders Robert Nixon and Stephen Lewis, both of
whose parties supported extension of aid to separate
schools, said that they hoped that it would not become an election issue. The Most Reverend Philip
Pocock, on behalf of the Roman Catholic Church,
regretted the government's decision but said that he
hoped that it would not become an election issue.
But it did become an issue despite everyone's

good intentions. There were, of course, good reasons for this. It had been an issue since before Confederation. In the B.N.A. Act the Protestant minority in Quebec and the Roman Catholic minority in Ontario were guaranteed the right to their "established" school systems. At that stage of history, education only went to Grade 8. With the extension of normal education to the end of Grade 13, two interpretations of the B.N.A. Act became possible. One was that the "established" school systems were those systems as established in 1863, that is, education until the end of Grade 8; the other was that the "established" school systems were the systems established for complete schooling, to whatever grade level that happened to be.

Practical consideration also played a role in the controversy during the election campaign. Since the public high schools were being changed from a graded to a non-graded system, transfer from separate to public high schools at the end of Grade 10 was thought by separate school supporters to be impractical.

Furthermore, Catholic separate schools did not receive the same degree of tax support as public schools, since they did not receive any corporate tax money. On the other hand, although the actual amount of support per student was greater in the public than in the separate schools, the percentage of support per student was higher for separate school students.

In opposing the further support of separate high schools, the government argued that their prime consideration was the value of a "single, universally accessible, publicly-supported secondary school system".

Furthermore, if aid were extended to separate secondary schools, the government pointed out that it would, in fairness, have to be extended to other religious groups such as the Jews and the Calvinists, both of which operated their own school systems supported merely by tuition and grants from their religious communities and both of which were pressing for public support.

During the election campaign, Davis found himself picketed by supporters of separate-school aid extension, especially students, everywhere he went. The issue that was not to be an issue blossomed.

In the election Davis's Conservative government was returned to office with forty-four per cent of the popular vote and a large majority of the seats. Only in the Windsor area was the Conservative party defeated by the issue of extended aid to separate schools.

- Should support for students in separate schools be extended past Grade 10? If all the subjects taught in regular public schools are taught in separate schools, should there be equal support per student? Should other minorities including Jews, Calvinists, individual non-denominational churches, and atheists receive support? Should private schools receive the same governmental support per student as regular public schools if they provide the same program?

- Is there any difference in principle, from the point of view of government funding, between a public school in which there is religious education and a separate school that provides the same academic program?
- Should the B.N.A. Act be revised to modify the right of Protestants in Quebec and Roman Catholics in Ontario? If so, on what principle?
- In the Ontario election, the extension of aid was criticized on the grounds that different religious groups would be discouraged from mixing with and understanding members in all groups in society. Do parochial or private schools tend to weaken in any way the unity of Canada? If so, how?

ANALOGY: "GOLD STARS AND BLACK MARKS".*
When their eight-year-old daughter, Avis, came home in tears each Monday from Fallsview Public School, near Niagara Falls, Mr. and Mrs. Peter Burnett felt a sense of helplessness.

Avis was crying because she had the longest row of black marks in the Grade Four classroom. During the Monday period of compulsory religious instruction the teacher asked each child about attendance at Sunday School the previous day. Those pupils who attended received gold stars; those who didn't got black marks. The idea sprang directly from Lesson Four, page 19 of the Grade Four Guide to

*By Pierre Berton, reprinted with permission from the Toronto *Daily Star,* January 10, 1961.

Religious Education: *Point of Contact: What did you do last Sunday? Collect varied information from members of the class.*

The Burnetts were new to Canada. They happen to believe that religion is a personal matter and that it is nobody's business how their children spend Sunday. They are Unitarians, but there was no Unitarian church in the area. "We weren't going to be blackmailed into going to another church merely for convenience," says Mrs. Burnett. And so, until they moved to a new neighbourhood, there were tears and hysteria every Monday morning because Avis knew she was going to get another black mark at school. . . .

Mr. and Mrs. Burnett did not learn until two years after the incident with Avis that they had the legal right to ask exemption for their child from religious instruction. . . .

- Is it necessary to have a government-approved guide on religious education in provinces where this subject is taught? Why?
- Should a government-approved guide suggest that teachers ask questions about what students did on Sunday? on Tuesday? What use could these questions have?
- Does the use of the guide referred to in the article violate the government policy that the program of religious education be made acceptable to all?
- Could religious education ever be made acceptable to all? If not, how would the government approval of the use of the guide be justified?
- Must a program of study be acceptable to all members of society?

THE ROLE OF GOVERNMENT

Ryerson and religious education

The problem of religious education in the schools of
Ontario has always been serious. When Egerton
Ryerson was Superintendent of Education in Ontario
between 1844 and 1876, it became critical. In his
report on education (1846), Ryerson devoted a
large section to the teaching of religion and morality.
Biblical history and morality were to be taught "without any restraint on one side, or any tincture of
secularism on the other". Ryerson attempted to
maintain a careful balance. On the one hand he
refused to make the Bible compulsory in the curriculum. On the other he threatened to resign when a
bill was passed through the legislature banning from
public schools all books containing controversial
dogmas or doctrines. That he was opposed to compulsory sectarian religious education in the public
schools led to his long dispute with Bishop Strachan;
that he was in favour of Biblical teaching is clear
from his having written *First Lessons in Christian
Morals for Canadian Families and Schools* to be used
as a text in the public schools. It is difficult to

decide whether Ryerson chose the reasonable position between the two extremes in religious education or whether his position summed up the ambiguities that the province of Ontario has always manifested about this controversial subject.

The 1944 program

In 1944 the minority Conservative government of George Drew introduced a program of religious instruction into the public schools of Ontario. This program was introduced through legislation that read, in part, as follows: "Subject to the regulations, two periods per week of one-half hour each, in addition to the time assigned to religious exercises at the opening of public school, shall be devoted to religious education.

"Instruction in religious education shall be given by the teacher in accordance with the course of study authorized for that purpose by the Department, and issues of controversial or sectarian nature shall be avoided.

"No pupil shall be required to take part in any religious exercise or be subject to any instruction in religious education to which objection is raised by his parents or guardians.

"The Minister may grant to a board exemption from the teaching of religious education in any classroom or school if the board requests in writing such exemption and submits reasons therefor."

This proved to be one of the most controversial

steps taken by a controversial government. By March of the next year, the Drew government found its very existence in jeopardy over this issue. The Liberals, under Harry C. Nixon, moved an amendment to a C.C.F. non-confidence motion as follows: "That the government has revised our traditional policy of non-sectarian public schools by introducing a programme of religious instruction which has caused disunity among large sections of our people, and has thereby violated the cherished democratic right of each to worship according to his conscience, free from interference by the State. . . ."

Late on the evening of March 22, 1945, the struggle over religious instruction reached its climax as the three party leaders, Mr. Nixon for the Liberals, E. B. Jolliffe for the official opposition, the C.C.F., and George Drew for the Conservative government, made their final statements.

Mr. Nixon argued that there was significant minority opposition to the program and that it would lead to an extension of the practice of establishing separate school systems along religious lines. Further, he was concerned that boards of education would have to consider the religious background of the teachers employed. For these reasons he and the Liberal Party opposed the program.

Mr. Jolliffe's central fear was that a basically religious issue would become a political football. To prevent this he urged C.C.F. members to vote according to their consciences and not along party lines. He personally opposed the new program and would vote against it because it weakened the roles of both church and state to so merge them.

The premier claimed that Mr. Nixon's fears were unsubstantiated, since any school board could opt out of the program and since the government was ready to review and revise the program so as to make it acceptable to all. The program was necessary, Mr. Drew said, for the training of future citizens. He gave the example of the British resistance to the Nazi menace as an illustration of the great significance of deep religious faith for a nation.

The C.C.F. party split in the voting and the amendment was defeated. Within two minutes, however, the Drew government fell on the C.C.F. non-confidence motion over another matter. But the legislation for religious education stood.

In the election that followed, Drew's Conservative party received an overwhelming majority. It seems that, if popular opinion is to be taken as a guide, the Conservatives had been vindicated.

The Issues

- Does any program of religious instruction violate the democratic human right of free worship? What reasons would you give in support of your answer?

Compulsory religious education in a democracy: majority v. minority

- If a large minority of citizens is opposed to the teaching of religion in public schools, should it be abolished? On what grounds is your view based?

- If a majority is opposed, should it be abolished?

ANALOGY. In the town of Oldview, ninety per cent of the residents are opposed to the teaching of history in public schools because they believe that the subject has no practical use and that the views presented in the history books make the past seen much worse than they would like to believe. However, a committee of teachers, psychologists, lawyers, and other professional experts have found that students who study history can think more clearly, are more self-assured, and make better citizens than those who do not study history.

- Should the minority of experts have the right to decide on the teaching of a subject over the protests of the majority?

- Who should decide whether fluorides should be put into the water supply of a town – dentists or the majority of citizens? Why? Should a minority opposed to fluoridation have the right to stop the addition of fluorides to the water supply?

- If a majority of residents are opposed on moral or religious grounds to the teaching of evolution, the presence of Negroes in the classroom, and the presence of boys and girls in the same classroom, should their will be respected in each case? Why? If only a minority is opposed, should its will be respected? What if the minority is forty-nine per cent of the population? one per cent of the population?

- Would you agree with the remarks of Mr. Nixon that the extension of the separate school system by minority religious groups establishing their own schools is undesirable? Why?

- Can one have a healthy democratic society when members are divided into many different religious groups? Can one have a healthy democratic society when all members hold the same beliefs? How would you justify your position?

Religious practices: tolerance in a democracy

- Which of the following religious practices should society tolerate: Jehovah's Witnesses doing missionary work door to door, attempting to persuade everyone of the correctness of their beliefs; Jehovah's Witnesses refusing blood transfusions for themselves on religious grounds; Jehovah's Witnesses refusing blood transfusions for their children; a satanic cult practising animal sacrifice; a cult advocating human sacrifice. What principles would you employ to decide on these matters?

Role of government in education

- Should boards of education ever consider the religious backgrounds of prospective teachers? If so, when and why?

- Would the religious background of a teacher be relevant if he taught: physical education; chemistry; mathematics; biology; English literature; religious studies?

- Should separate schools (Roman Catholic) be permitted to consider the religious backgrounds in the hiring of all of its teachers? of any of its teachers? Or should only educational qualifications be considered?

- Should non-sectarian private schools be permitted to consider the religious backgrounds of candidates for teaching positions?

- Should the political background of a teacher be considered in hiring him? Why?

- Should any of the following be rejected as teachers: a member of the Communist party; an atheist; a racist; a person with a criminal record; a man living common-law with a woman, or vice versa; an alcoholic; an ex-convict who had been convicted of a sexual offence; a user of marijuana; a member of a radical separatist group like the F.L.Q.? What reasons could you give to justify your answers?

- Would you agree with Mr. E. B. Jolliffe that the government should have nothing to do with religion? On what grounds?

- Should political parties take positions on religious issues, or should such issues simply be matters of personal conscience? Why?

- Do you believe that the roles of both church and state are weakened by a program of religious education in the public school? How would one or the other suffer? Could either or both gain support from the other? How?

- What control, if any, should governments exert on public schools, especially in the following areas: religious studies; moral education; literature; biology; mathematics? What control, if any, should governments exert on separate schools in these areas?

- If a specific program is considered worthwhile for students in general, should individual school boards be allowed to decide whether the program should be introduced?

- Should individual school boards have been permitted to opt out of the religious education program in Ontario? What reasons do you have for taking this position? If an individual school board could opt out, would it solve the problems of all or any individuals or minority groups in the system?

- Should the school board be permitted to make similar decisions about: a new mathematics program; an established physics program; a driver education program?

- If you had been a member of the Ontario Legislature in 1944, how would you have voted? Why would you have voted this way?

Function of religious education

- Do you believe that one of the goals of education should be the training of future citizens?

- Is a program of religious education necessary for citizenship education?

- Do you believe that deep religious faith helps one to defend his freedom? On what grounds do you base your belief?

- Was the British resistance to Naziism in the Second World War dependent on a deep religious faith, as Premier Drew claimed?

PARALLEL SITUATIONS. Would the following situations weaken Mr. Drew's position? Would they influence your position in any way?
- In 1943, the defenders of Stalingrad and Leningrad succeeded in repelling the overwhelming German attacks on their cities despite the great

odds against them. Yet most, if not all, of their leaders were atheists.

- In the twelfth and thirteenth centuries there arose a religious group called the Cathars, or Albigenses, in southern France and northern Italy. The Cathars believed in chastity, poverty, and piety. The leaders of this sect renounced meat, wine, sex, and privacy. All members were profoundly moral with deep religious commitment. They were, however, considered by the Church to be heretical, especially because of their rejection of the doctrine of an afterlife.

  In 1208 the Pope demanded an Albigensian Crusade. In 1209, 20,000 knights with foot-soldiers began a systematic destruction of Cathar cities. The heretics either recanted or were burned to death. In 1244 the last Cathar stronghold, Montsegur, fell, and giant bonfires around the palisades burned the last 200 Cathars to death.

The Jackson case: clergymen in schools

It is not an easy decision for parents to have their children exempted from classes in religious education, for the child may be led to feel that he is "different". Mr. and Mrs. Jackson of Etobicoke, Ontario, made this difficult choice for their son. Early in 1963, Mrs. Jackson began to wonder whether the decision was worthwhile when she discovered that on two occasions at regular school assemblies at Heatherbrae School clergymen had spoken on religious matters. Upset, she contacted Dr. Preuter, the Superintendent of Schools. Mr. Sager, a trustee, replied by citing the legislation concerning school visitors and that concerning exemption from religious education. This did not satisfy Mrs. Jackson, since children could hardly be exempted from regular school assemblies.

The section of the Public Schools Act reads as follows: ". . . every clergyman is a school visitor in the municipality where he has his pastoral charge.

"School visitors including clergymen may visit Public Schools, may attend any school exercise, and at the time of the visit may examine the progress of the pupils and the state and management of the schools and give such advice to the teachers and pupils and any others present, as they deem expedient."

- Does official government recognition of clergymen as "school visitors" in any way violate either the letter or the spirit of the law that permits exemption of students from religious education?
- If not, do you believe that all clergymen should be recognized as school visitors in their areas? Why?
- Who should be recognized as school visitors: trade union leaders; business executives; all political candidates; poets; police officers; government leaders? Can you suggest anyone else?

The Mackay Report: The Report of the Committee on Religious Education in the Public Schools of Ontario 1969

In January 1966, by an order-in-council, a committee was established on religious education. Its terms of reference were: "to examine and evaluate the present programme; to receive representations from all interested bodies about the effectiveness and desirability of the programme; to consider suggestions for changes and improvement; to study means by which character building, ethics, social attitudes and moral values and principles may best be instilled in the young; to consider the responsibility of the Public Schools in these matters; and to make recommendations thereon for the information and consideration of the Minister."

More than three years later, in February 1969, after numerous meetings throughout the province at which 141 written briefs were presented, the committee released its findings and recommendations. Among the major recommendations of this committee are the following:

(1) The abandonment of the present program of religious instruction and its aims.

(2) The repeal of the regulation allowing boards of education to choose the type of sectarian teaching to be given in schools within its jurisdiction. Therefore, it would no longer be possible to have one school in a district presenting a sectarian Protestant program, a second in that same district presenting a sectarian Jewish program, and a third presenting a sectarian Roman Catholic program.

(3) The repeal of the legislation making clergymen official school visitors (see page 99).

(4) The retention of opening exercises consisting of the National Anthem and prayers of a nonsectarian nature, but elimination of Bible reading.

(5) A program of moral development to be integrated into the entire curriculum and into extra-curricular activity.

(6) Optional courses in world religion in Grades 11 and 12.

Consider your position on each of the major recommendations of the Mackay Report:

- Should the aims of the present program of religious education in Ontario be revised? Should the operation of the program cease?
- Should boards of education no longer be permitted to decide which type of sectarian teaching is to be given in which schools within their jurisdiction?
- Should clergy continue to be official school visitors?
- Should Bible reading be entirely eliminated in the schools? Should opening exercises consisting of the National Anthem and prayers of a non-sectarian nature be retained?
- Should moral education be included in the school program? Should it be integrated into any discipline or topic of study where the discussion of moral questions can be initiated?
- Should optional courses dealing with world religions be given in Grades 11 and 12? Should they be given earlier?

Final consideration

- What further recommendations would you make concerning the teaching of such controversial matters as sex, politics, religion, and ethics?

BIBLIOGRAPHY

Beck, Clive. *Moral Education in the Schools*. Toronto: the Ontario Institute for Studies in Education, 1971.

Beck, C. M.; Crittenden, B. S.; and Sullivan, E. V., eds. *Moral Education: Interdisciplinary Approaches*. Toronto: University of Toronto Press, 1971.

Breasted, Mary. *Oh! Sex Education!* New York: Praeger Publishers, 1970.

Carter, Francis G. *Judical Decisions on Denominational Schools*. Toronto: Ontario Separate School Trustees' Association, 1962.

Fellman, David, ed. *The Supreme Court and Education*. New York: Bureau of Publications, Teachers College, Columbia University, 1960.

Girvitz, Harry K., ed. *Contemporary Moral Issues*. 2nd ed. Belmont, California: Wadsworth, 1968.

Holt, Simma. *Sex and the Teen-Age Revolution*. Toronto: McClelland & Stewart, 1967.

Johnson, Warren R. *Human Sexual Behavior and Sex Education*. 2nd ed. Philadelphia: Lea & Febiger, 1968.

Lawrence, Jerome; and Lee, Robert E. *Inherit the Wind*. New York: Bantam Books, Random House, 1964.

Levin, M. A.; and Eisenberg, J. A. *Dilemma*. New York: Holt, Rinehart & Winston, 1971.

Nelson, Jack; and Roberts, Gene. *The Censors and the Schools*. Boston: Little, Brown, 1963.

Parker, Donald; O'Neil, Robert M.; and Econopouly, Nicholas. *Civil Liberties: Case Studies and the Law*. Boston: Houghton Mifflin, 1965.

Phillips, C. E. *Religion and Our Public Schools*. Toronto: Ethical Education Association, 1961.

Powers, G. Pat; and Baskin, Wade. *Sex Education: Issues and Directives*. New York: Philosophical Library, 1969.

"The Present Status of Sex Education in Canadian Schools". Canadian Education Association, Research and Information Division. Toronto: September 1964.

Price, Neil G. *Education – Religion – Politics in Ontario*. North Bay: Northland Printers, 1966.

Religious Information and Moral Development. Report of the Committee on Religious Education in the Public Schools of the Province of Ontario. Toronto: Ontario Department of Education, 1969.

Rich, John. *Catching Up With Our Children*. Toronto: McClelland & Stewart, 1968.

St. John, J. Bascom. *Separate Schools in Ontario*. Toronto: Roman Catholic Bishops of Ontario, 1963.

Silcox, C. E. *Religious Education in Canadian Schools*. Toronto: Committee on Religious Education in Schools, Department of Christian Education, Canadian Council of Churches, 1960.

Sissons, C. B. *Church and State in Canadian Education*. Toronto: Ryerson Press, 1959.

Sizer, Theodore R., ed. *Religion and Public Education*. Boston: Houghton Mifflin, 1967.

Tucker, Bernard, ed. *Catholic Education in a Secular Society*. London: Sheed & Ward, 1968.

Wiebe, R. H. *Peace Shall Destroy Many*. Toronto: McClelland & Stewart, 1962.

FILMS

The Merry-Go-Round. 23 minutes. Black and white. NFB. An examination and discussion of what young people are saying and doing about sex.

Teaching: A Question of Method. 6 minutes. Colour. Available from the International Film Bureau Inc., 332 South Michigan Avenue, Chicago, Illinois 60604. During class a teacher states that in his opinion the Christian Bible is not necessarily true. The mother of one of his students complains, maintaining that the teacher has no right to cast doubts on beliefs that she has tried to inculcate in her daughter. The audience is asked to make a decision.

CBC AUDIO TAPES

Children and Evil. 30 minutes. Examines both fairy-tales and the results of child psychology to find out what some of the most important influences are in the development of a child's first ideas about good and evil.

Disappearing Boundaries in Theology. 3 tapes, 30 minutes each. Three talks on the altered meaning of the word "religion"; the disappearance of the boundary between religion and secularity; the relation between religion and phenomenology and psychotherapy, the "death of God" phenomenon.

Looking East for Light. 4 tapes, 30 minutes each. Talks on why Buddhism, Hinduism, Taoism, and Eastern religions and philosophies hold such attractions for young North Americans today.

Political Film. 1 hour. The history and uses of political film.

Sex Education and Family Life. Catalogue Nos. 553-555.

The Two Histories. 30 minutes. Canadian history is taught differently in Ontario or British Columbia from the way it is taught in French-speaking Quebec. Several college students, half originally French-speaking, illustrate that there are at least two stereotyped models of Canadian history.

Venereal Disease. 1 hour. A program about the growing problem of V.D. and the possible solutions.

MORDECAI RICHLER

"The Street"

The bestselling Canadian author is at his gamey, full-flavoured best in this lively account of his childhood in Montreal. The story overflows with the rich humour and perception that has made Richler Canada's best-known living novelist.

"Hunting Tigers Under Glass"

In this book, which won a Governor General's Award, Richler turns his ironic eye to the facts of life around him – from Expo 67 through Norman Mailer, Jews in sport, Tarzan of the Apes, and numerous other stopovers – and finds them as strange as anything in fiction. So he coldly and mordantly shoots them down.

"DRUGS, SOCIETY AND PERSONAL CHOICE"

by Drs. Harold and Oriana Kalant

This book aims to put into the sharpest possible focus questions of fact and matters of value judgment, and how the two interact. The authors' purpose is to encourage the type of discussion that the LeDain Commission has requested and that the subject fully deserves. Both authors are associated with the Addition Research Foundation in Toronto.

"THE PURSUIT OF INTOXICATION"

by Dr. Andrew I. Malcolm

This book examines the many reasons why people have used and continue to use the psychoactive drugs. These are considered under five main headings: religion, medicine, endurance, extinction, and recreation. Dr. Malcolm also touches on his theory regarding the alienating influence of such illusionogenic drugs as marihuana and LSD.

"YOUR NAME AND COAT-OF-ARMS"

by The Rev. James S. McGivern, S. J.

This book explains the origin and gives some of the intriguing history behind hundreds of our most frequently occurring family names. Some 1,250 surnames common in Canada are indexed, and for many of them the book shows the crests and coats-of-arms traditionally associated with the names.